Enjoy this
true story.
Best regards,
Gene Crumley
1-3-17

Inky's Great Escape!
Dr. Gene Crumbley

This book belongs to:

_____

Dedication

Dedicated to one close friend and several other friends who shared their enthusiasm and interest in this book. I am deeply grateful and indebted to each one for their encouragement and suggestions and their time and effort in helping with the editing process.

Copyright © 2016 by Dr. Gene Crumbley

All rights reserved. No part of this book may be reproduced or transmitted in any form or by any means, electronic or mechanical, including photocopying, recording, or by any information storage or retrieval system without permission in writing from the copyright owner.

For additional copies of this book visit:
www.genecrumbley.com
www.amazon.com
www.barnesandnoble.com

ISBN- 978-0-692-76950-8

Inky's Great Escape!

Dr. Gene Crumbley

Illustrations by
Blueberry Illustrations

Inky was an octopus
That was kind of small,
Just about as big as
A little soccer ball.

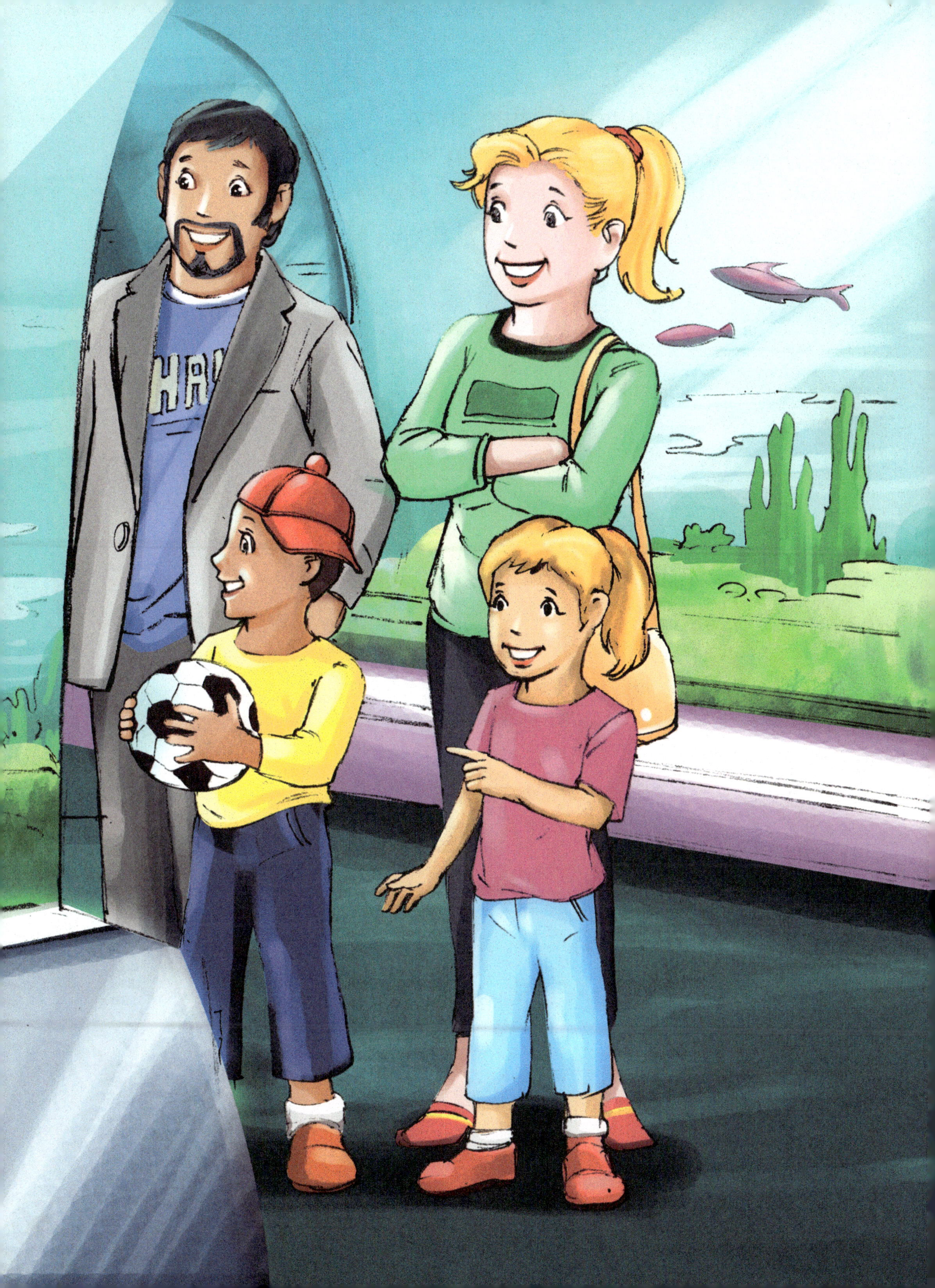

They had named him Inky
'Cause at times, quick as a wink,
If frightened, he squirted a liquid
That was as black as ink.

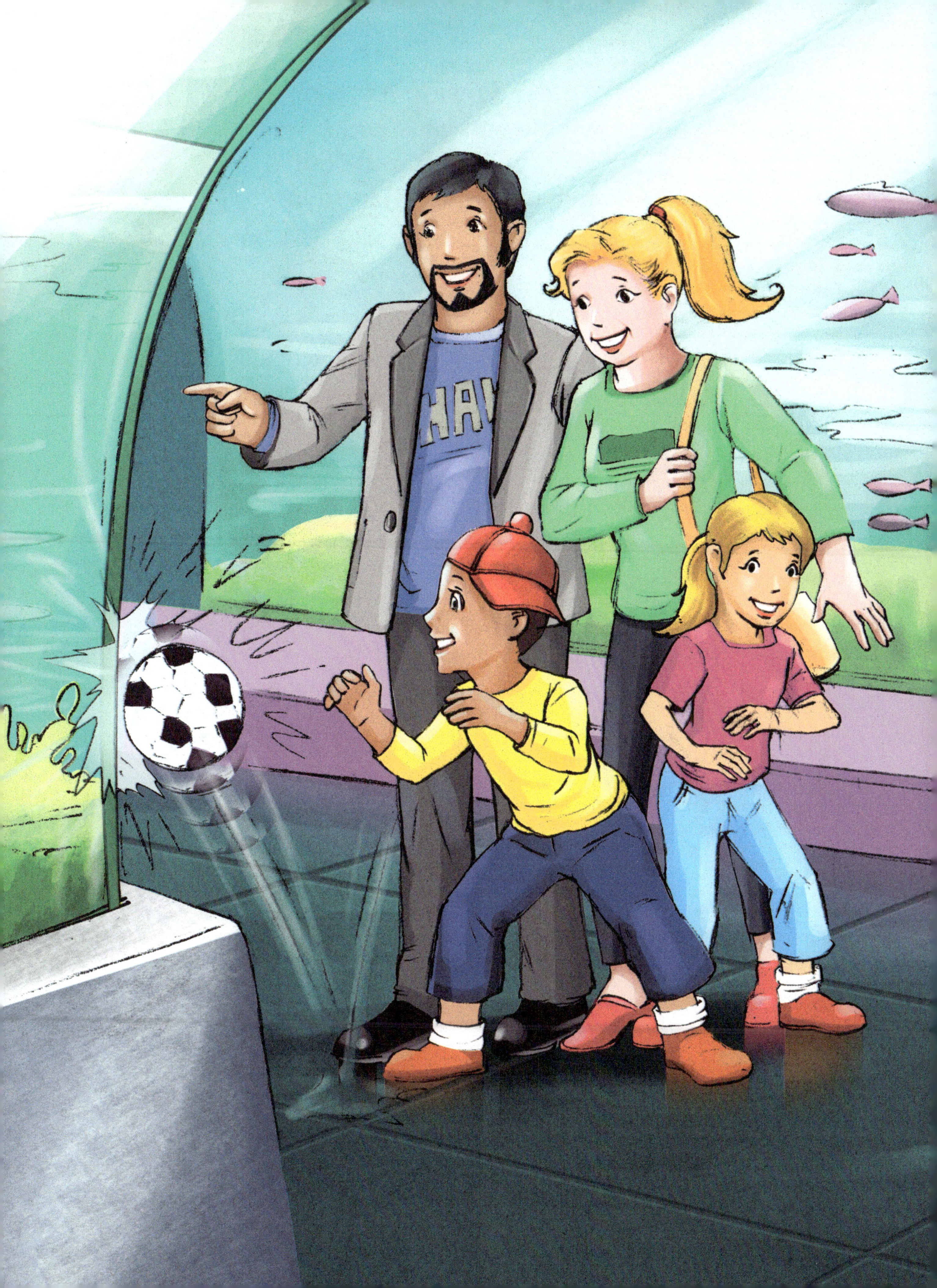

Inky played inside his tank
Just like human girls and boys,
Tossing a ball back and forth
And playing with other toys.

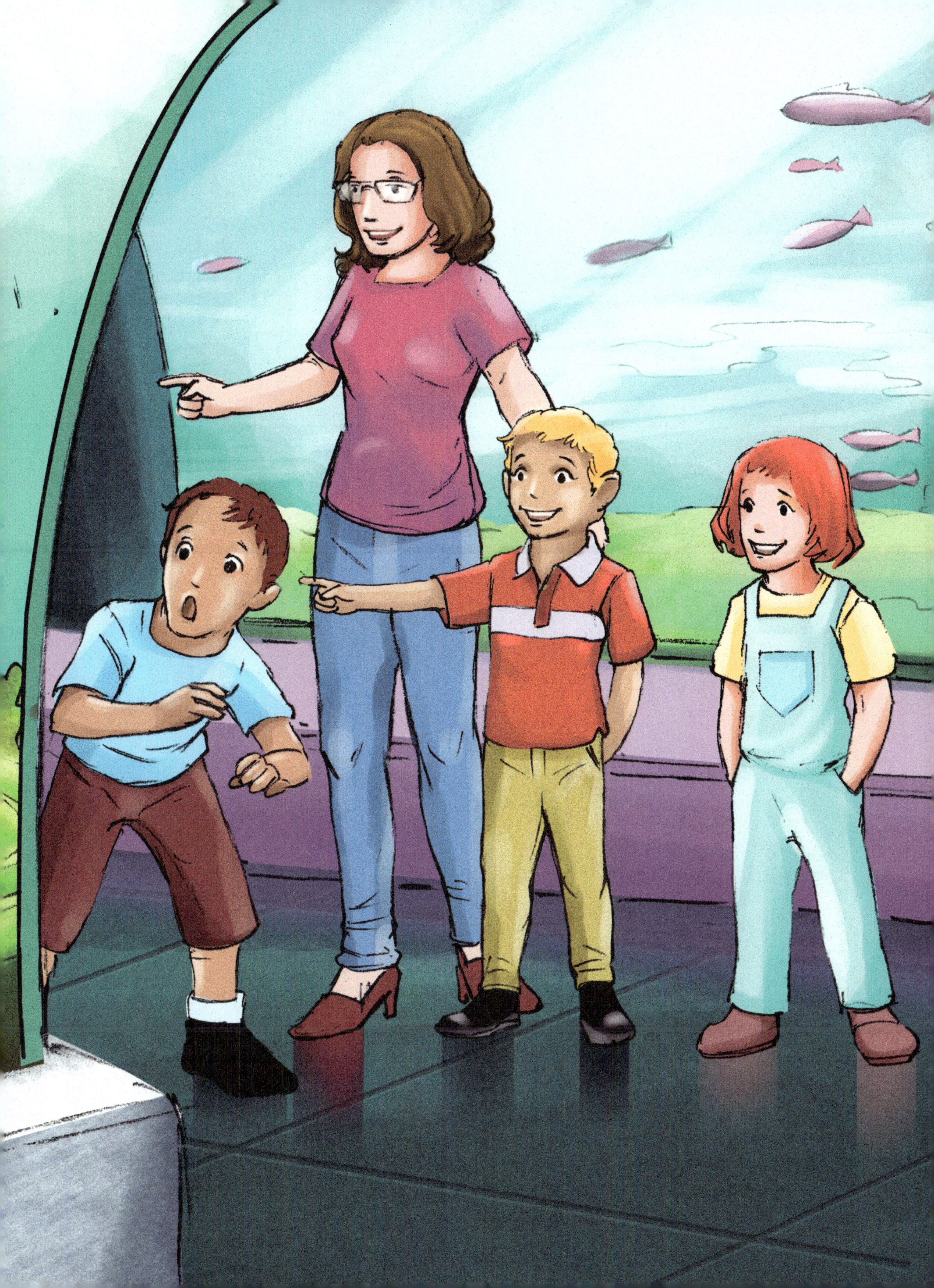

Inky was very curious
And was anxious to see more,
Of the ocean he saw outside
That had a rock lined shore.

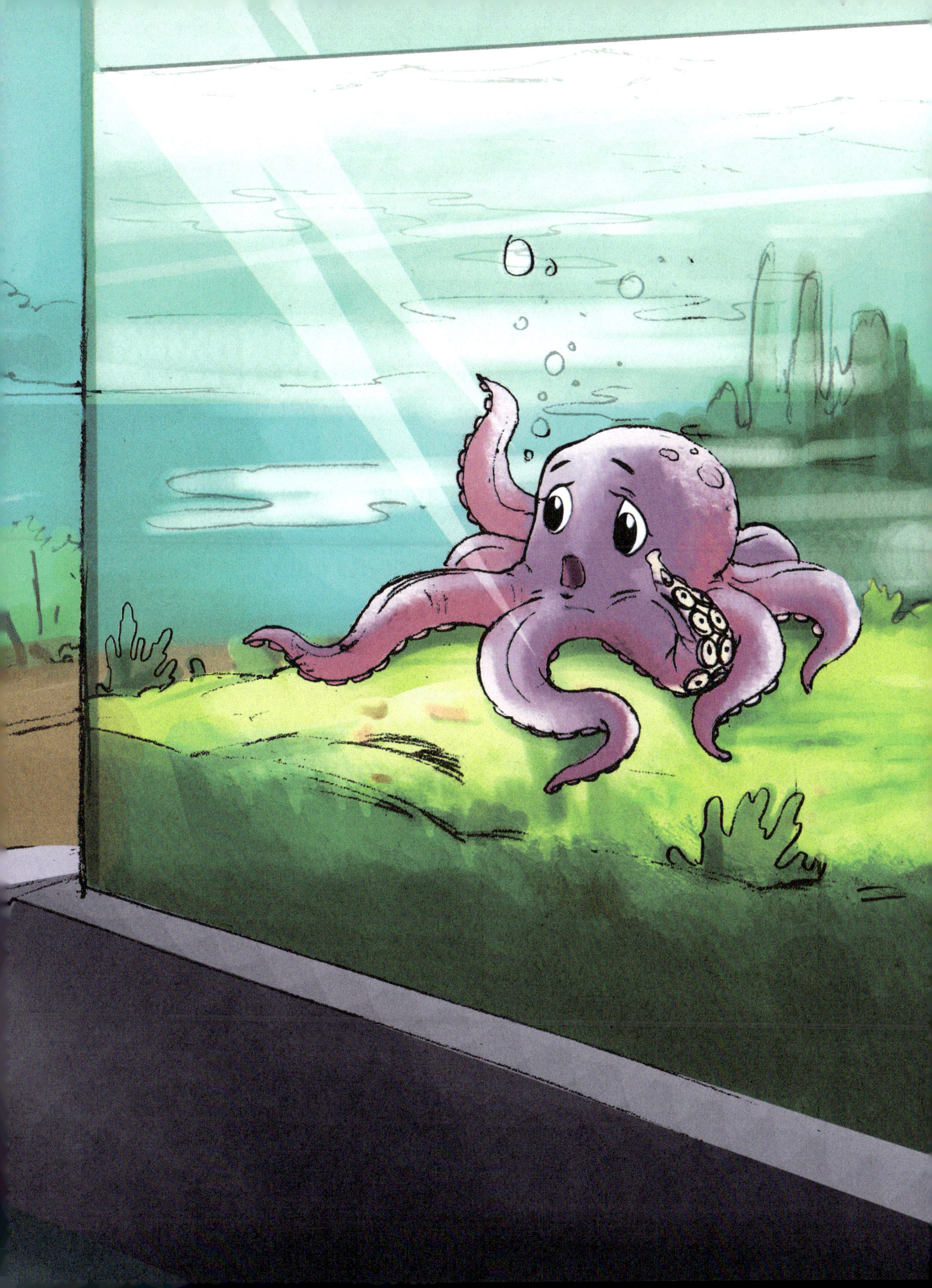

Inky looked up and saw a hole
And it was a lovely sight,
For he knew he could get through it
And escape into the night.

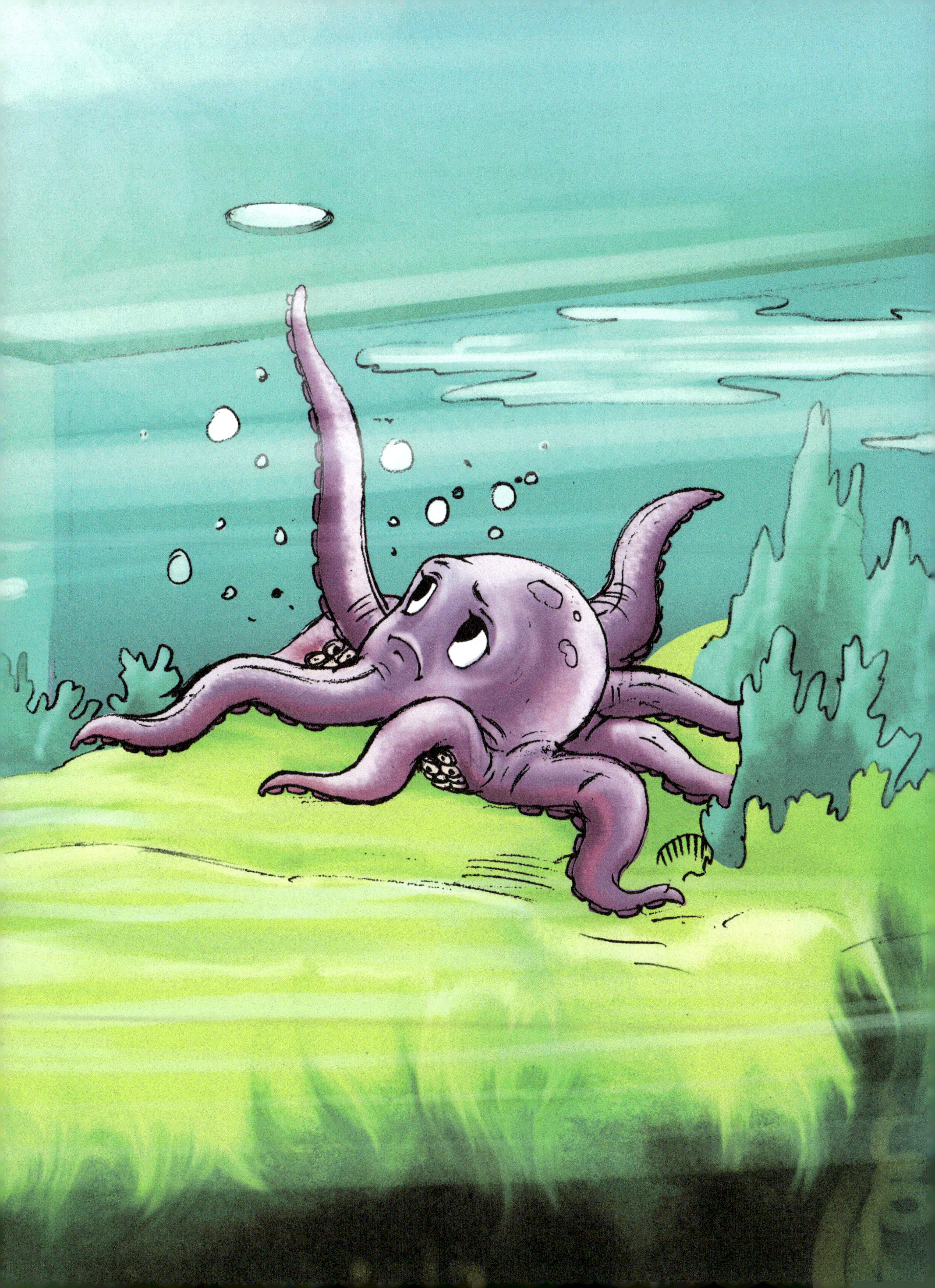

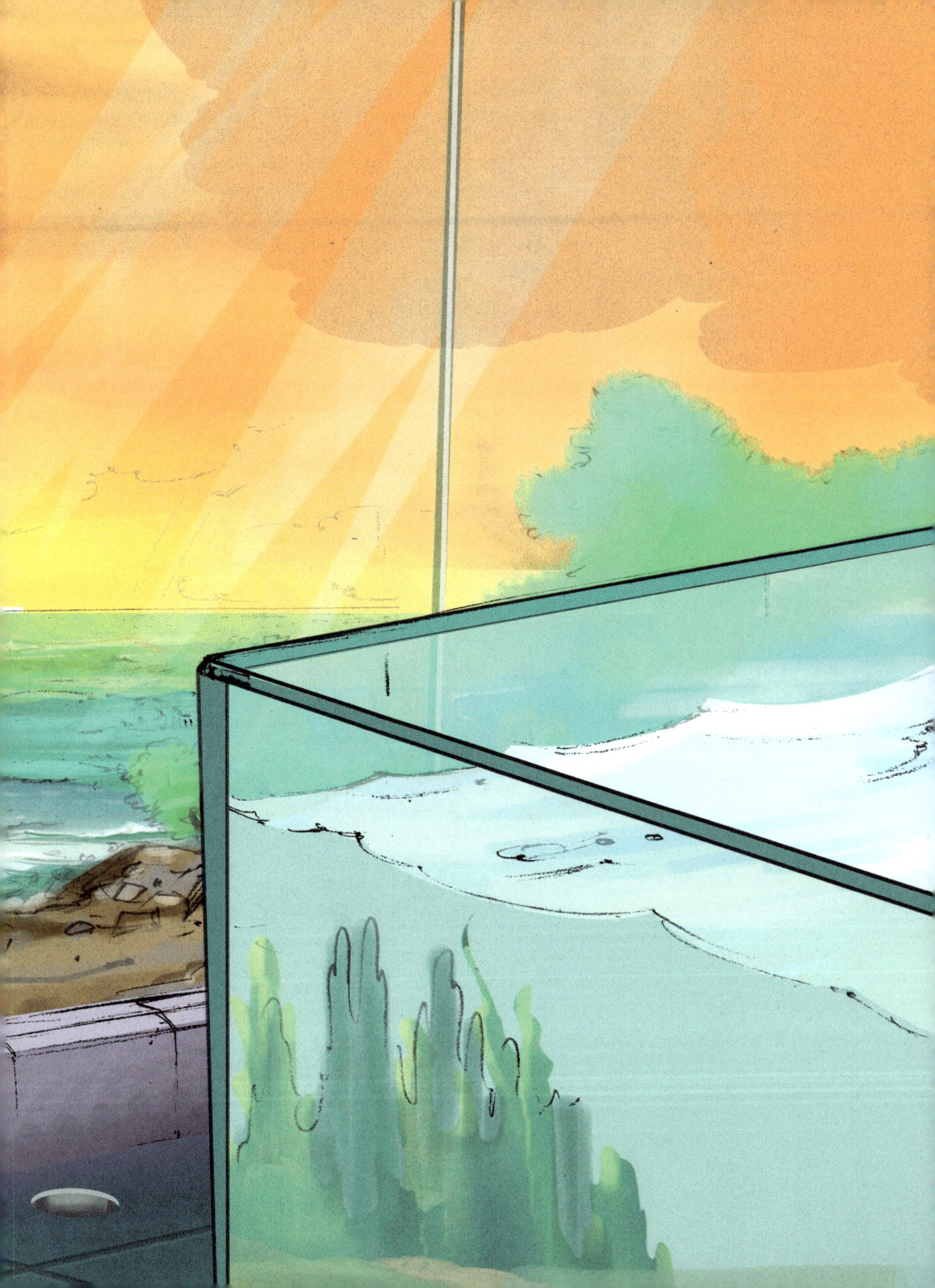

Inky reached up with one arm
That was long and strong
And squeezed through the hole;
Was Inky doing wrong?

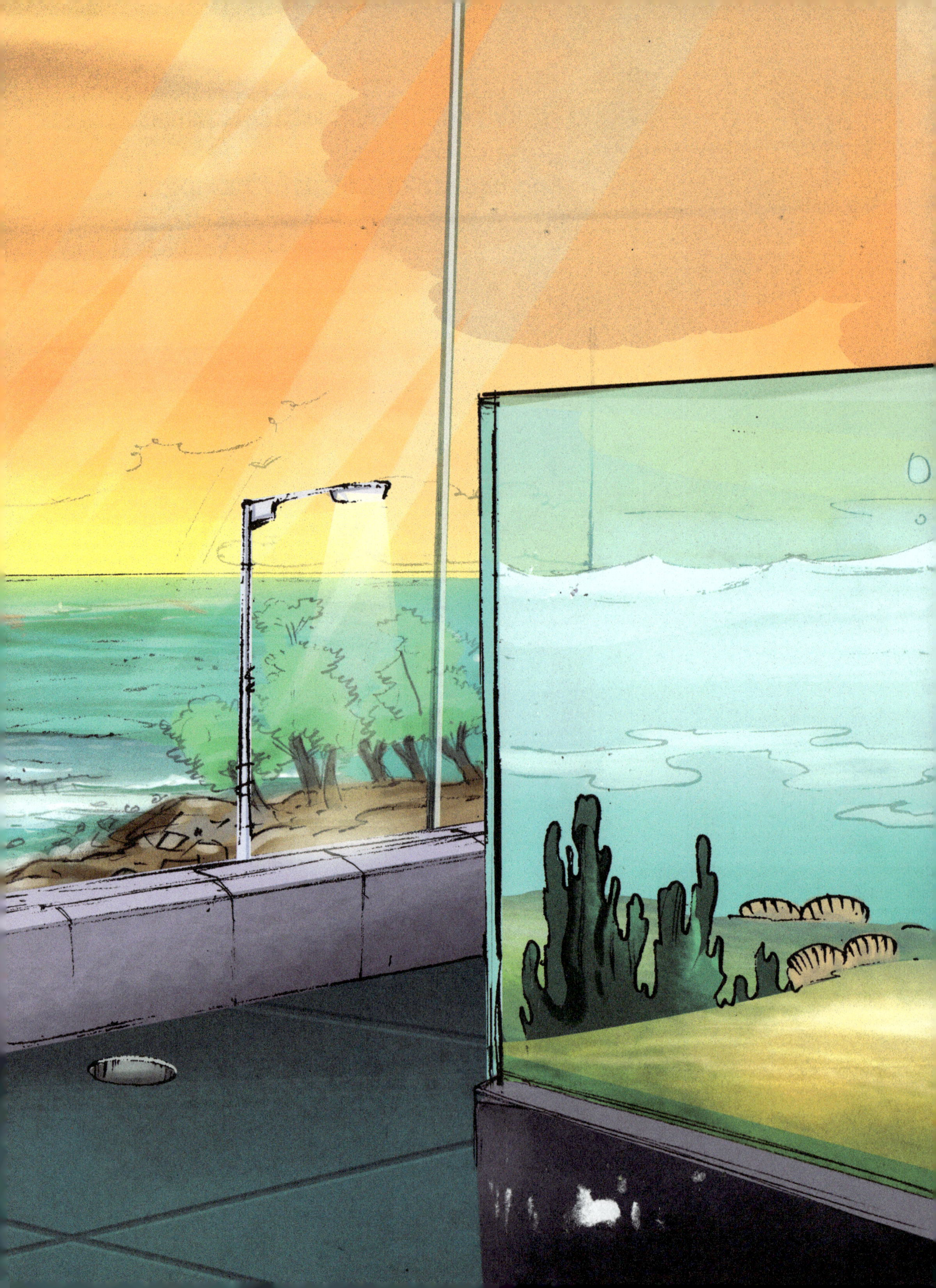

Inky was now outside the tank,
Moving slowly down its side;
His arms had many suckers
So he did not slip or slide.

There was a drainpipe in the floor
That was six inches round
And Inky crawled over to it
Without making any sound.

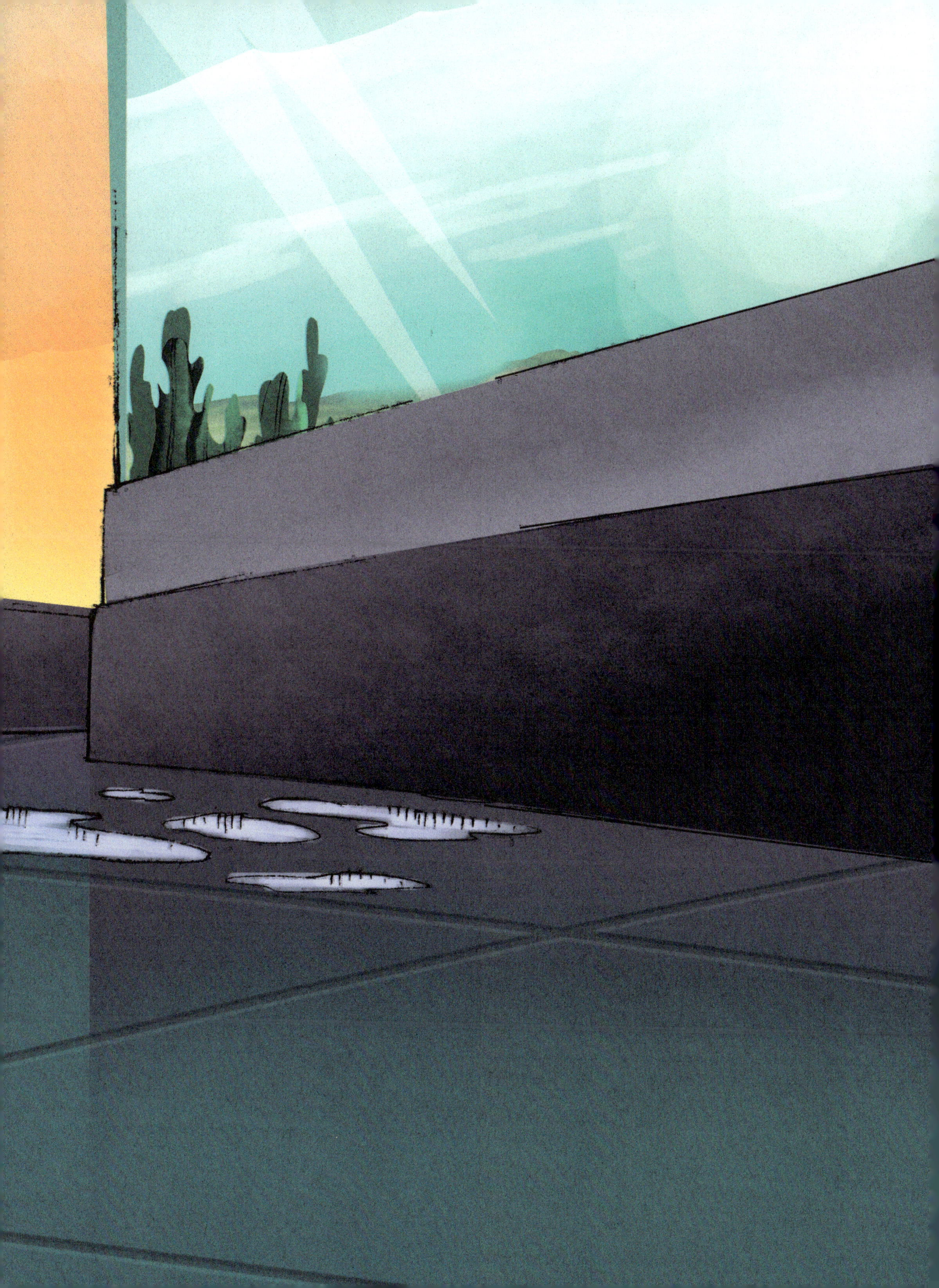

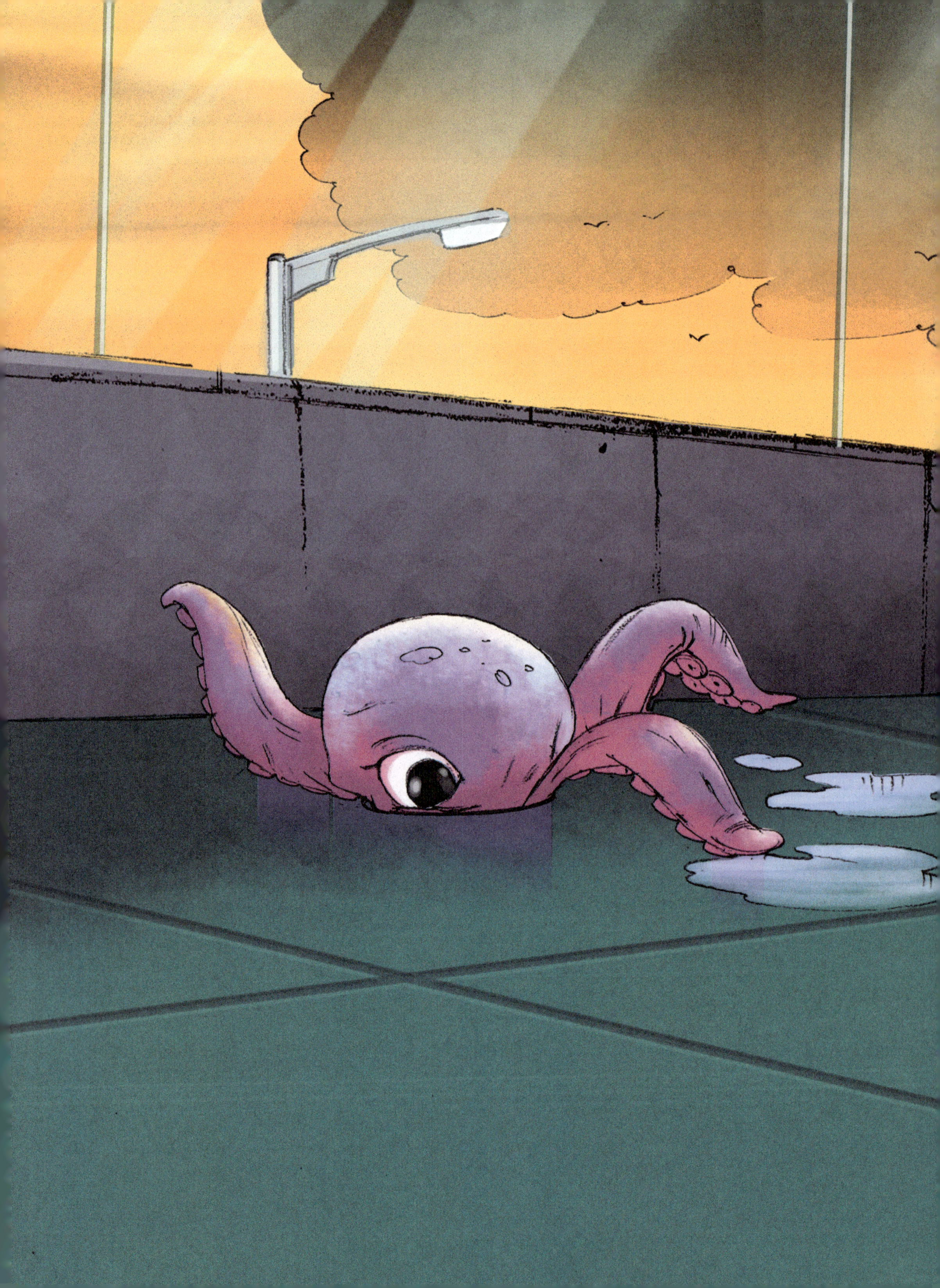

Inky got into that pipe
And quickly worked his way
To the very end of it
Where it over looked the bay.

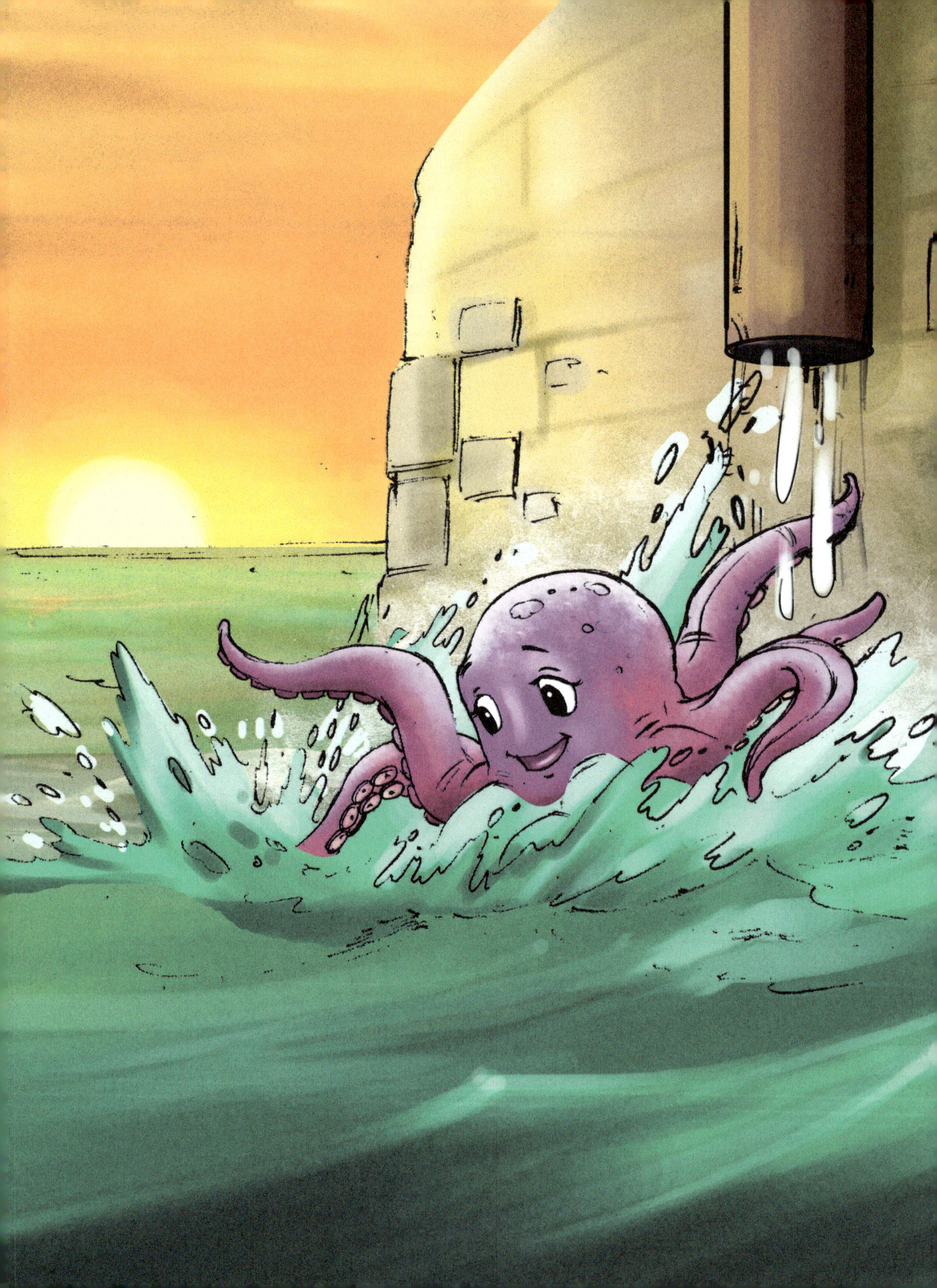

He hit the water with a splash,
And now that he was free,
Inky must have thought,
"They never will catch me."

Next day the workers came
And found wet tracks on the floor,
Then cried out, "Where is Inky?"
The octopus they all adored.

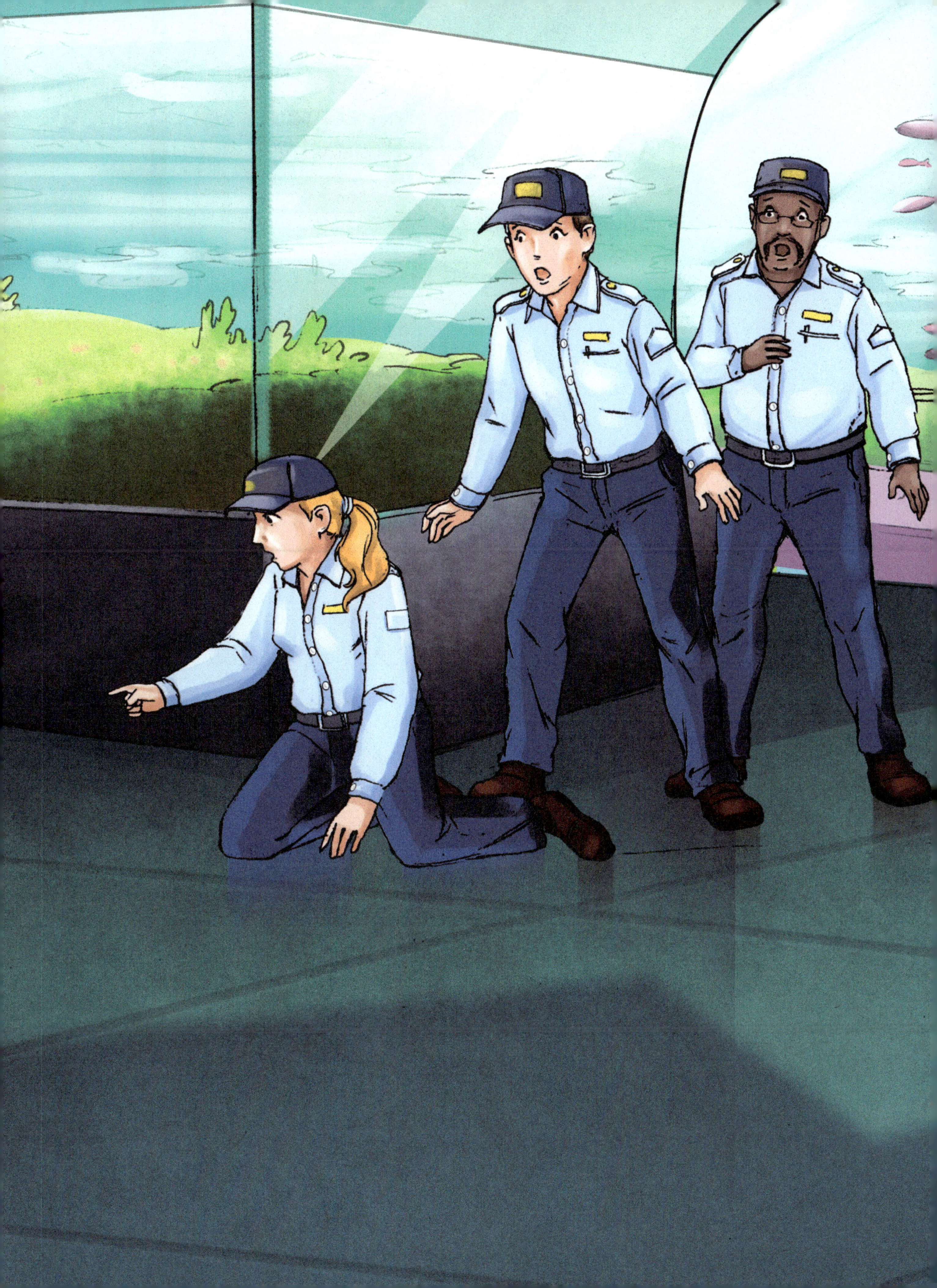

They all were broken-hearted
And couldn't understand why
Inky didn't leave a note,
Or take the time to wave good-bye.

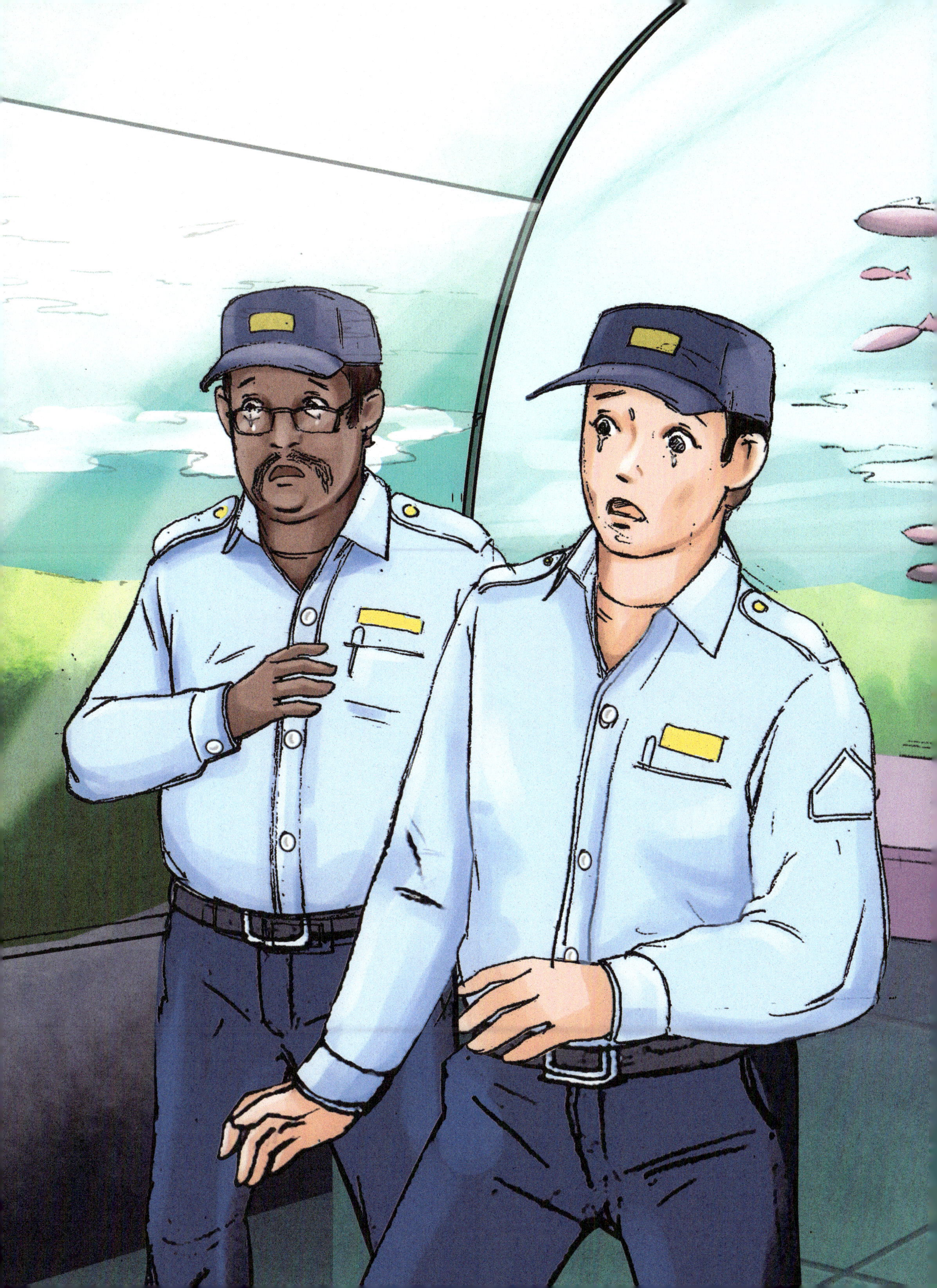

But Inky did turn and wave,
Then with a smile on his face,
He swam out to the ocean
To find a brand new place.

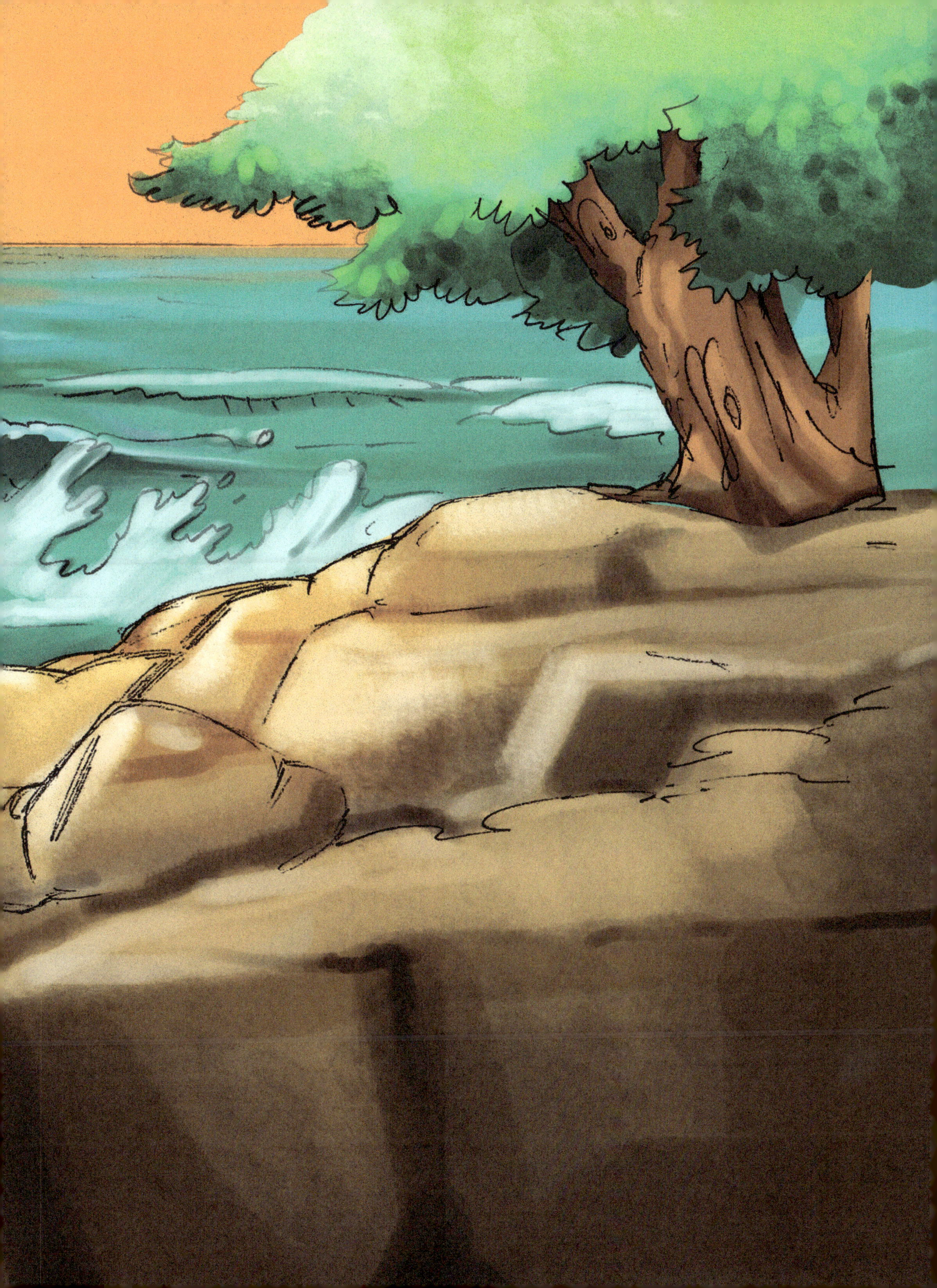

Inky is now in his new home
Where he got to on the sly.
He's with other octopuses
Who all love this little guy!

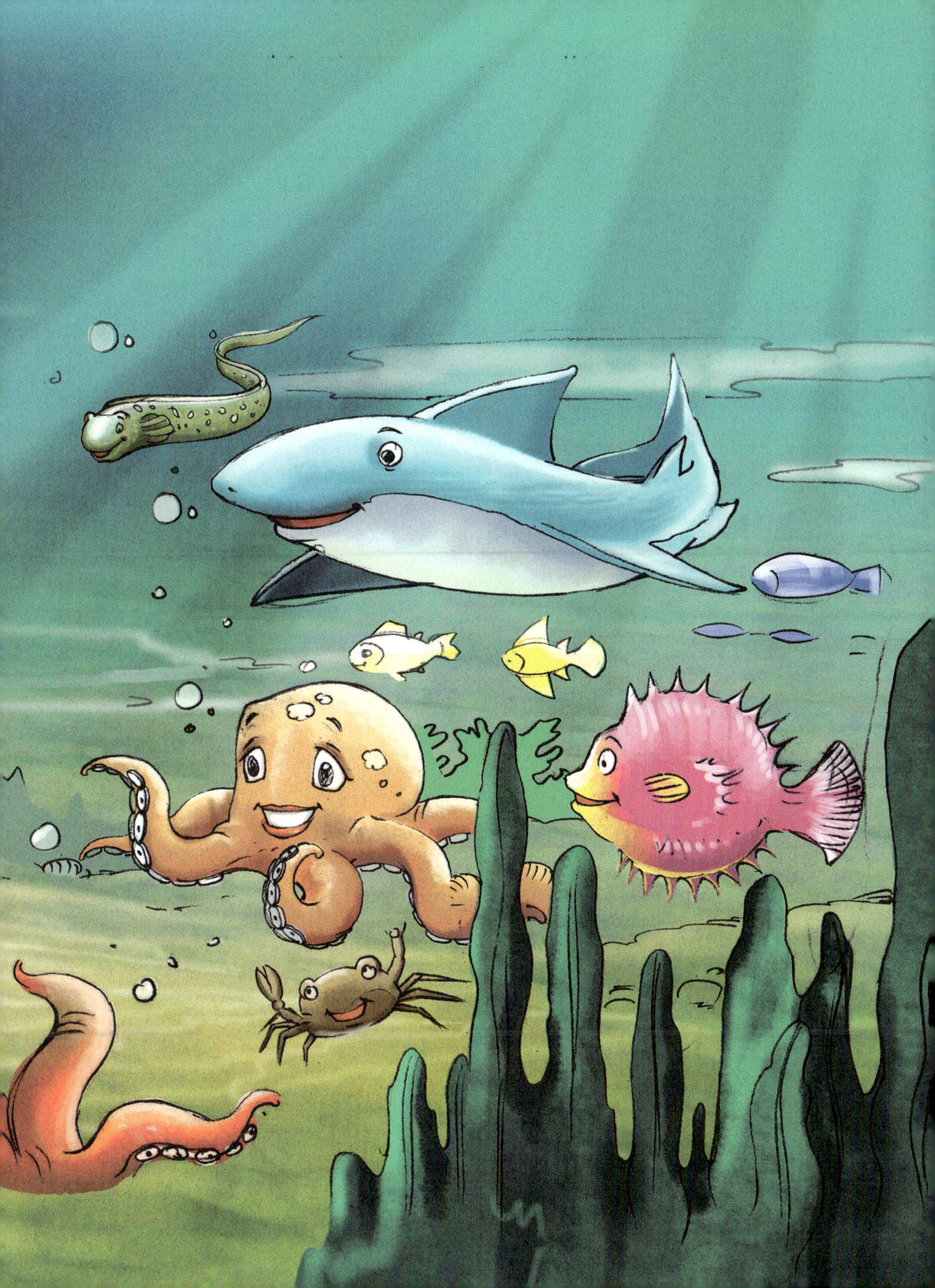

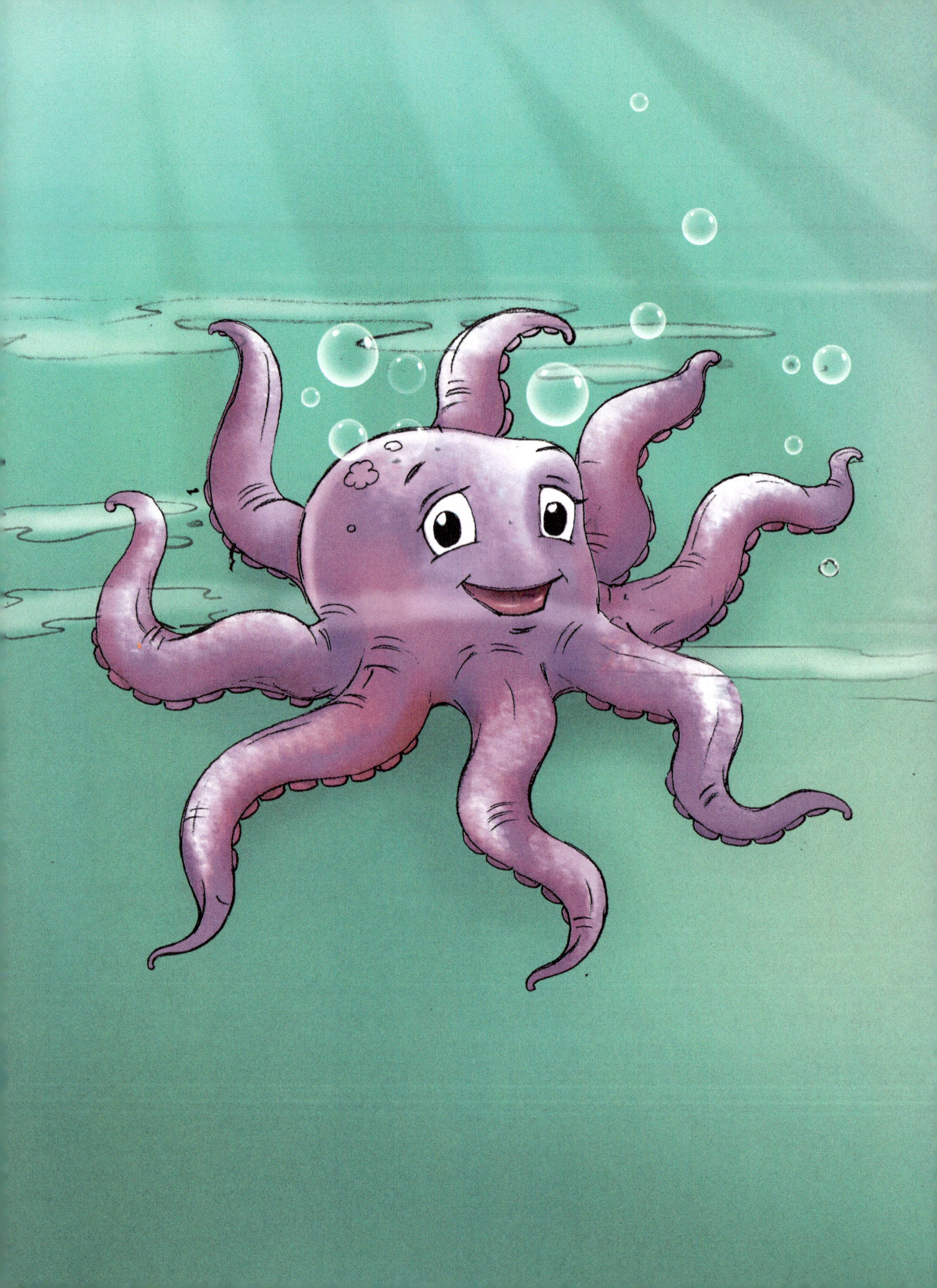

If you happen to run across Inky,
Relax, don't make a big fuss.
For even though he is well-armed,
He's very sweet, not dangerous!

The End

Interesting facts about Inky and other octopus of the same kind:

When you see two or more octopuses,
Calling them octopi is amiss;
Because in some cultures
People are much offended by this.

Inky has three hearts,
One for his body and head
And one for each of two gills,
And his blood is blue---not red.

Inky also has nine brains,
One for each arm, all eight,
And just one for his head and body,
So his intelligence is great!

Inky can solve small problems,
Like unscrewing the lid from a jar,
And if he could get to one,
He might open the door of a car.

Inky also changes colors
When predators come around.
This gives him good protection
For he blends in with his background.

Inky can build a fortress
With rocks and sea shells;
Sharks swim by and don't see him
Because he is hidden so well.

Inky's body is soft and spongy
So this should come as no surprise,
He can squeeze into a coconut shell
And all you'll see are his two eyes.

One more thing about Inky,
He can scoot 25 miles per hour
By gushing water through his gills.
Can this be "sea" horsepower?

About the author

Gene Crumbley is a retired Doctor of Chiropractic who has four children, twelve grandchildren and four great grandchildren. After retiring in 1998 at the age of 70, he became interested in photography and began taking pictures of the many birds seen by him in his backyard and other places. He also developed an interest in writing and wrote and self-published four books.

Currently he is completing a book for children about birds, with pictures and descriptive poems about each.

Some of his other interests include writing poetry, playing golf, woodworking, and making greeting cards and tea coaster tiles with his bird pictures and other images.

His self-published books, cards and tea coasters can be seen on his website at www.genecrumbley.com

CPSIA information can be obtained
at www.ICGtesting.com
Printed in the USA
LVOW06*0354201216
518048LV00007B/10/P